One Quiet Page
A Gentle Writing Companion

Tracey Power Hilborn

The Curiosity Cabinet Press

One Quiet Page
A Gentle Writing Companion
Copyright © 2026 by Tracey Power Hilborn
All rights reserved.

No part of this book may be reproduced, stored, or transmitted by any means—electronic, mechanical, photocopying, recording, or otherwise—without written permission from the publisher, except for brief quotations used in reviews, critical articles, or educational contexts.

Published in the United States by:
The Curiosity Cabinet Press
www.thecuriositycabinetpress.com

ISBN: 978-1-967930-05-0

Our books may be purchased in bulk for educational, promotional, or business use.
For ordering inquiries, please contact:
orders@thecuriositycabinetpress.com

Printed in the United States of America
(The printer and distributor may vary by region.)

Introduction

This is not a book that asks much of you.

You don't need to be a writer.
You don't need to know what you want to say.
You don't need to start at the beginning or finish at the end.

These pages are here for the moments when your mind feels full, or tired,
or simply in need of somewhere to rest for a while.

Each prompt lives on a single page for a reason.
You are not meant to hurry.
You are not meant to explain yourself.
You are not meant to fill every space.

Some days, you may write a few lines.
Some days, a sentence.
Some days, nothing at all.

All of that counts.

This book isn't a plan or a practice.
It's a place to pause —
to notice what's already here,
and to let the page hold it for you.

Take one quiet page.
That's enough.

How To Use This Book

There is no right way to move through these pages.

You can begin anywhere.
You can skip what doesn't speak to you.
You can return to the same page more than once.

Each prompt is meant to stand on its own.
You don't need to build toward anything.
You don't need to remember what you wrote before.

If a page feels heavy, you're allowed to stop.
If a page feels quiet, you're allowed to stay longer.
If words don't come at all, that's not a failure —
it's part of the listening.

You don't need to write in full sentences.
You don't need to make sense.
You don't need to explain yourself.

This book works best when you let it be small.
One page.
One moment.
One honest line, or none at all.

Close the book whenever you need to.
It will be here when you come back.

Start Where You Are

Write exactly what is on your mind right now.
Not what should be there.
Not what sounds interesting.
Just this moment, as it is.

If your mind is noisy, let it be noisy on the page.

Something You've Been Carrying

There is something you've been holding longer than you meant to.
You don't have to explain it.
You don't have to solve it.

Just write what it feels like to carry it.

A Small Relief

Write about something small that eases you, even briefly.
A habit.
A place.
A sound.
A moment.

Nothing big.
Nothing life-changing.
Just enough.

What You Wish You Could Say

Write what you haven't said —
to a person,
to yourself,
or to no one in particular.

You don't have to send it.
You don't even have to reread it.

Today, in Ordinary Detail

Describe today without commentary.
No judgments.
No lessons.

Just what happened.
Just the facts.
Let the meaning, if any, find you later.

A Question You're Not Ready to Answer

Write the question that keeps circling.
The one you don't have an answer for yet.

You're not required to respond to it here.
Let the page hold it for a while.

Something That Still Lingers

It might be a moment.
A conversation.
A look.
A season.

Write about what stayed after everything else moved on.

What You're Tired Of

This is not a complaint.
It's an acknowledgment.

Write honestly about what you are tired of carrying, fixing, managing, or pretending.

Stop when you're ready.

A Small Hope

Not a plan.
Not a promise.

Just something you hope might happen —
even if you're not sure you believe it yet.

Write it anyway.

Something That Waits

There is something in your life that hasn't moved yet.
It isn't rushing you.
It isn't gone.

Write about what it's like to know it's still there.

A Place You Feel Slightly More Yourself

This can be a real place or an imagined one.
Somewhere you exhale without thinking about it.

Describe it the way it feels, not the way it looks.

What You Miss (Without Explaing Why)

You don't need to justify this.
You don't need to make it reasonable.

Just write what you miss.

A Sentence You Need to Hear

Write a sentence you wish someone would say to you. Then write it again, as if it were already true.

Something You're Learning Slowly

Not something you've mastered.
Not something you can explain yet.

Just something that's unfolding, one small realization at a time.

A Moment You Didn't Know Mattered

It seemed ordinary at the time.
Maybe it still does.

Write it anyway.
Let the page decide what it holds.

What Feels Heavy Right Now

You don't have to name the cause.
You don't have to fix it.

Just write where you feel the weight.

Something You've Outgrown

This doesn't have to be dramatic.
It can be a belief, a habit, a role, or a season.

Write what it's like to stand on the other side of it.

A Small Truth

Not a life lesson.
Not a revelation.

Just something you know, quietly and without debate.

What You're Protecting

It might be a hope.
A boundary.
A piece of yourself.

Write about what you're keeping safe — and why it matters.

A Time You Felt Understood

You don't need to recreate the whole story.
Just the feeling of being seen.

Write from that place.

Something You're Allowing Yourself Now

Rest.
Change.
Joy.
Distance.

Write what has shifted — even slightly.

What You're Afraid to Rush

There are things that shouldn't be hurried.
This might be one of them.

Write about what deserves time.

A Question You Ask Yourself Gently

Not the sharp ones.
Not the demanding ones.

The kind you ask when you're being kind to yourself.

Leave This Page Unfinished

Begin writing and stop before you feel done.
Mid-thought is enough.

You can return later — or not.
Either way, the page will remember.

What You're Holding Gently

There is something you're being careful with right now.
Not because it's fragile —
but because it matters.

Write about how you're holding it.

A Moment of Almost

Something nearly happened.
Something almost changed.
Something almost mattered more than you expected.

Write about the almost.

What Feels Safe Today

Safety can change from day to day.

Write about what feels safe right now,
even if it didn't yesterday.

Something You Trust Without Proof

Not because it's logical.
Not because it's guaranteed.

Just because it feels steady.

Write about that kind of trust.

A Version of You That Still Visits

Not the one you are now.
Not the one you used to be all the time.

The one that appears in flashes.

Write when they show up.

Something That Quietly Sustains You

It doesn't ask much of you.
It doesn't announce itself.

Write about what keeps you going in small, unnoticed ways.

A Last Word

If you reached this page, you don't need to feel finished.

This book was never meant to be completed,
only visited.

Some pages may be full.
Some may be half-written.
Some may still be waiting.

All of that is enough.

You don't have to keep everything you wrote.
You don't have to understand it yet.
You don't have to do anything with it at all.

What mattered was the pause.
The noticing.
The moment you gave yourself a place to land.

When you're ready, you can close the book.
Or you can turn back to any page and begin again.

There will always be another quiet page.

About

This book was created by someone who believes that writing doesn't have to be productive to be meaningful.

It doesn't have to turn into anything.
It doesn't have to be shared.
It doesn't have to prove that you're good at it.

It only has to give you a place to pause.

One Quiet Page belongs to a larger, quiet way of approaching writing — sometimes called the quiet writer — where the work is not to produce, but to notice.

The work behind *One Quiet Page* comes from a long love of words, margins, old notebooks, and the small moments where something unspoken finally finds a way to the page.

If this book met you where you were, that was its only job.

You can find other quiet projects, prompts, and printed companions at **The Curiosity Cabinet Press**, where books are made to be kept, not rushed.

Made in the USA
Coppell, TX
22 February 2026

72109540R00023